A BOOK OF BRIDGES

HERE TO THERE AND ME TO YOU

Written by Cheryl Keely

Illustrated by Celia Krampien

Bridges do more than connect one place to another.

They bring the whole world together.

They can be wooden-covered,

Hartland Bridge, in Canada, is the world's longest covered bridge. It is about as long as 36 school buses and crosses the Saint John River from Hartland to Somerville, New Brunswick.

The Golden Gate Bridge in California is one of the world's most famous suspension bridges. It opened in 1937 and isn't actually golden, but orange. The architect chose the color orange because it is distinct from the colors of the sky and sea, making it easier for passing ships to see.

golden-gated,

or in London, falling down.

London Bridge was the first stone arch bridge built in Britain. It crosses the River Thames. It has undergone many renovations over the years and is now made of concrete and steel.

Some bridges are moveable, going up and Up and UP,

Drawbridges are bridges that open and close. They date to medieval times, when knights in armor—and dragons?!—fought for their castles. Today, drawbridges open up to let boats and ships pass.

before coming back down.

While others are simple, stones—

Stone bridges can be as simple as a few stones placed across a shallow stream. This is sometimes known as a clapper bridge. Or they can be complex structures such as South America's Puente de Piedra in Lima, Peru, which crosses the Rímac River. It is known as the Bridge of Eggs because the mortar used in building the bridge was mixed with bird eggs to make it stronger.

placed one, two, three
—to make a safe crossing.

Bridges just for animals help them find new homes,

new friends, and plenty of food.

Banff National Park in Canada has the most wildlife bridges in the world. The crossings allow animals—such as bears, wolves, moose, and lynx—to safely cross roads and highways.

And trains can use bridges to clickity-clack along, carrying people to people. Family together again.

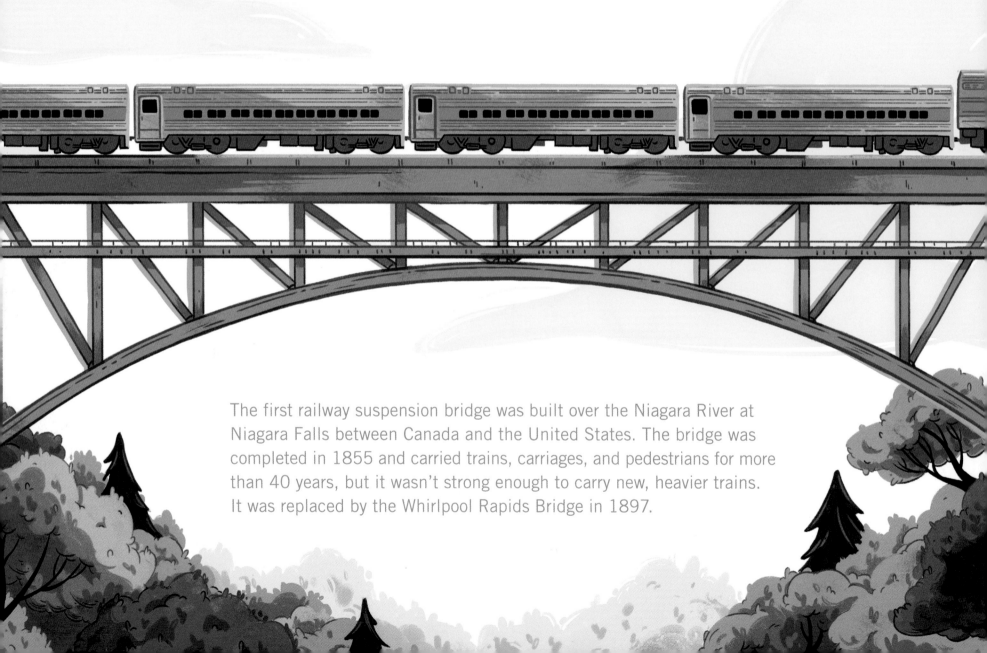

The first railway suspension bridge was built over the Niagara River at Niagara Falls between Canada and the United States. The bridge was completed in 1855 and carried trains, carriages, and pedestrians for more than 40 years, but it wasn't strong enough to carry new, heavier trains. It was replaced by the Whirlpool Rapids Bridge in 1897.

Some bridges join country to country,

The Three Countries Bridge at the borders of France, Germany, and Switzerland only truly connects France to Germany. But Switzerland is only a hop, skip, and a yodel away!

making a big world seem smaller.

Or connect neighborhood
to neighborhood,

turning strangers into friends.

The Brooklyn Bridge crosses New York City's East River to connect Brooklyn to Manhattan. Days before the Brooklyn Bridge opened, P. T. Barnum led 21 elephants over it to prove that it was safe.

Some bridges are rickety, ratchety, swinging and swaying their way to beautiful, hidden away places.

Bridges made of vine and rope are among the earliest types of bridges. They can be scary to cross because there isn't much to them—the rope can be as skinny as your arm.

Bridges can be made
by bending backward

and stretching and stretching

until all fall down, laughing.

And rainbows make bridges from sunshine to rain.

A rainbow is not really a bridge. It is an arc of colors formed in the sky when sun shines through drops of water.

But the bridge I like the best
isn't so grand.

It connects me to you and you to me . . .
through the simple holding
of hands.

To Dad, for still sending rainbows, and Mom, for all the hand-holding you do

—Cheryl

✿

For Mom and Dad

—Celia

Sleeping Bear Press®
2395 South Huron Parkway, Suite 200
Ann Arbor, MI 48104
www.sleepingbearpress.com

Printed and bound in the United States.

10 9 8 7 6 5 4 3 2 1

Library of Congress Cataloging-in-Publication Data

Names: Keely, Cheryl, 1969- author. | Krampien, Celia, 1988- illustrator.
Title: A Book of Bridges : here to there and me to you /
written by Cheryl Keely ; illustrated by Celia Krampien.
Description: Ann Arbor, MI : Sleeping Bear Press, [2017] | "Bridges are some
of the most fascinating structures in our landscape. "From towering suspension
bridges to humble stone crossings, this book visits them all in sweet, bouncing text
with expository sidebars. But while bridges can be quite grand, this reminds us
that their main purpose is bringing people together"—Provided by the publisher.
Audience: Age 4-8.
Identifiers: LCCN 2016030976 | ISBN 9781585369966
Subjects: LCSH: Bridges—Juvenile literature. | Bridges—
Social aspects—Juvenile literature.
Classification: LCC TG148 .K44 2017 | DDC 624.2—dc23
LC record available at https://lccn.loc.gov/2016030976